Annika
and the
Emperor Penguin

Author Reputation Press LLC
45 Dan Road Suite 36
Canton MA 02021
www.authorreputationpress.com
Hotline: 1(800) 220-7660
Fax: 1(855) 752-6001

Ordering Information:
Quantity sales. Special discounts are available on quantity purchases by corporations,
associations, and others. For details, contact the publisher at the address above.

Printed in the United States of America.

ISBN-13:   Softcover   978-1-951020-36-1
           eBook   978-1-951020-37-8

Library of Congress Control Number: 2019912011

Annika
and the
Emperor Penguin

Gail Borkosky

AuthorReputationPress
Creativity & Branding

"Wake up! Today's the day we dock!"

Annika could not contain her excitement as she raced to the window squinting from the glare of the sun streaming through the small port hole. Grace rubbed her eyes and slowly rose from her bed, yawning. She padded across the room in her bare feet. Surrounded by the Southern Ocean, with mountains of ice bobbing in the waves, the girls watched as a bird soared overhead.

Annika was learning about the wildlife that live in the Antarctic at school and she desperately wanted to see them in their natural habitat. For Annika's birthday, as promised by her parents, she set sail on a cruise to a place she had only read about in books—the South Pole. Grace had been Annika's best friend from the time they were born. They went to the same school and played together almost every day, and there was no one else Annika would rather share this special holiday with.

Although December is the start of summer at the South Pole, the air remains cold and the ground stays covered in ice and snow. The girls dressed in their warmest clothes and donned hats, scarves, boots, and mittens. Annika's parents, in the adjacent cabin, had given the girls permission to explore as long as they did not wander too far from the ship and they promised to return in time for dinner.

Annika and Grace stood on the deck waiting for the cruise ship to come to a complete halt. They watched as the fur seals played in the surf below and a snow petrel swooped under the water only to reappear with a fish in its mouth. The girls were warned not to bother the animals they came in contact with but to stand at a safe distance and simply observe their behavior.

Once on solid ground, it became clear to Grace that there was not much to see other than miles of ice and snow. "Where are all the animals?" she asked. "Where are the polar bears?"

"Polar bears don't live at the South Pole, silly. They only live at the North Pole, but if we're fortunate, we might find the emperor penguins I've been reading about!" Annika proclaimed.

While the girls walked along the shoreline, Annika told Grace all she had learned about the penguins. "Emperor penguins are the tallest penguins in the world," she explained, "and they only live at the South Pole. Although penguins have feathers and wings, they cannot fly, and they will migrate over sixty miles just to find a mate. After the mom lays an egg, the dad will keep it safe and warm while the mom goes looking for food. When the egg hatches and the mom returns, they reunite as a family."

Grace was so intrigued by the story of the emperor penguin that she did not watch where she was stepping and tripped over a deep crack in the ice. She started to slide into the crevasse, but Annika quickly pulled her up by the arms and dragged her to safety. "Wow, that was close!" exclaimed Grace.

"Quiet, did you hear that?" whispered Annika pressing a finger to her lips.

The girls listened closely. There was a faint sound coming from the bottom of the crevasse. It sounded very much like someone was crying. Annika and Grace carefully crawled to the edge of the crack and peered into the opening.

"Who's there?" yelled Annika for there was not much light where the sound was coming from.

"Penny," came a small voice in return.

"Are you hurt?" asked Grace.

"No," said Penny, "but I can't get out. Will you help me?"

The girls knew they had to do something to help Penny, so they put their heads together and came up with a plan.

"Take your scarf off and tie it to mine," said Annika. "We can lower it down to Penny and use it to pull her out of the crevasse."

Grace tied the two scarves together and lowered them down to Penny. "Tie it around your waist," instructed Grace, "and we'll pull you out."

Penny tied the scarves around her, and Grace and Annika slowly and steadily elevated her out of the crack. When Penny was pulled to safety, all three girls collapsed on the ice to catch their breath.

"Who are you?" inquired Annika when the girls had finally recovered.

"I'm Penny Penguin and I've been down in that crevasse since last night. I fell in while walking with my colony and now I don't know where they are," whined Penny.

Both girls looked at each other and smiled. "Are you an emperor penguin?" asked Annika still smiling.

"Yes," said Penny, "I'm an emperor penguin. Why?"

"We have just set out to look for the emperor penguins. We'd be happy to help you find your family," said Annika while Grace nodded in agreement.

Penny was very grateful for the kindness of her new friends, and the three of them walked hand in hand while Annika explained how she and Grace had arrived at the South Pole.

The girls were so focused on their conversation that they were taken by surprise when a very large and very wet seal emerged from the icy waters. *Roar!* Came the sound as he towered over the girls. *Roar!* Came the sound again. Penny jumped back in fear for she had heard that sound before.

"Who are you?" asked Annika confused.

"I am Liam, a leopard seal, and you are trespassing on my territory," said the seal.

Penny knew that leopard seals like to eat penguins for dinner and she started to tremble. She hid behind the girls and wrapped the scarves around her head hoping the seal would not notice her.

Annika stepped forward and confronted Liam. "We didn't mean to disturb you, Mr. Seal. Our friend has been separated from her family and we are trying to find them," explained Annika while pointing to Penny.

"Do you know where they might be?" asked Grace. Penny reluctantly peeked through the scarves wrapped around her face and met the seal's eyes.

"Yes, I have seen them," said Liam looking back at Grace, "but before I let you pass you will have to give me something in return. My head gets cold when I am out of the water and your warm hat might be just the thing I'm looking for."

The girls looked at each other and shrugged their shoulders, puzzled by Liam's strange request. Grace quickly removed her hat and put it on Liam's head. Liam smiled and gave a sigh of relief.

"Ah, much better," breathed Liam. "If you continue walking toward that mountain of ice, you will find your colony," said Liam nodding toward the ice glacier in the distance. "You may pass." And he disappeared back into the water with a big splash.

The girls continued on their journey but when they reached the site where the penguins should have been, all they saw was more ice and snow. Penny sat down and began to weep for she was tired and missing her family.

"Don't cry," said Grace hugging Penny. "We won't give up until we find them."

"That's right," agreed Annika. "Someone around here must know where they are."

Just then, an elegant albatross gracefully swooped down and landed on Grace's head.

"Who are you?" asked Annika chuckling to herself, for the sight of Grace with a large bird on her head was quite amusing.

"My name is Abigail and I've come to see if I can offer you some assistance. You appear to be lost."

"We are looking for our friend's family and they seem to have disappeared. Have you seen them?" asked Annika.

Penny was still on the ground with the scarves piled on her head as Abigail looked her up and down.

"Remove your scarves so I may see you better," said Abigail.

Penny stood up and slowly removed the scarves from her head as Abigail eyed her once more.

"If you are looking for a colony of emperor penguins, then yes, I have seen them," declared Abigail.

The girls became excited again and Penny jumped for joy. "Where are they?" she squealed.

"I will tell you if you give me something in return," said Abigail gazing this time at Annika. "My children have nothing to keep them warm at night while they sleep. Your big fluffy mittens might be just the thing I'm looking for."

"Take them!" exclaimed Annika as she quickly removed her mittens and handed them to Abigail.

"Thank you," said Abigail. "Continue your journey for you have not walked far enough. If you go to the next glacier, you will find your family on the other side." And she spread her enormous wings and flew away carrying a red fluffy mitten in each foot.

Determined to find the emperor penguins, Annika, Grace, and Penny continued to trudge along the ice and snow. Their feet were getting sore and they were tired and hungry, but they refused to give up.

It seemed like they had been walking for hours when they finally reached the glacier where Abigail had directed them. As they turned the corner, they stood motionless with open mouths and wide eyes. Standing before them were hundreds—rather thousands—of penguins gathered on an enormous ice floe.

Penny started to jump up and down and clap her flippers in excitement.

"We found them! We found them!" she exclaimed.

"But there are so many. How will we ever find your parents?" asked Grace bewildered.

"That's easy!" said Penny. "Each family uses a variety of unique vocal sounds in order to contact each other. I'll walk through the crowd making that sound and my parents will hear me."

Annika looked at Grace, doubtful that the plan would work. Since neither of the girls had any other ideas, they began to follow Penny through the crowd. They could barely hear Penny above the noise of the other penguins, but she was persistent as she weaved through the colony.

After a short while, Annika could hear the same noise Penny was making from far off in the distance. The girls abruptly stopped and looked at each other in disbelief.

"You heard it too?" asked Annika.

"Yes!" cried Grace and Penny in unison. "This way!"

The girls hurried as they followed the sound and quickly found themselves standing in front of two beautiful emperor penguins. They were very large with a white belly and sleek black head and backside. Each had a pale yellow breast and bright yellow patches around their ears. Their necks were very graceful as they lowered their heads to gaze at the girls.

"Penny!" shouted her mom. "I thought you were lost forever," she said as she kissed the top of Penny's head. "How did you ever find us?"

"Mom, Dad, these are my friends, Annika and Grace. They are here on holiday and found me stranded in a deep ice crevasse. They have been helping me find my way back to you ever since," explained Penny.

"It's very nice to meet you," said Penny's mom to Annika and Grace, "and thank you for bringing our Penny back to us. How can we ever repay you?"

"You're welcome," replied Annika, "and it's nice to meet you too. We really need to head back to the cruise ship before my parents start to worry. We promised to be back before dinner, but I don't know how we'll ever make it in time," said Annika pointing worriedly to the ship in the far distance.

"I can help you with that," declared Penny's dad. "Wait here." And he disappeared into the water. Moments later he returned followed by a very large humpback whale. The whale gently laid his head on the ice and his eyes twinkled from the light of the sun.

"Hi, I'm Henry and I hear you need a ride back to your ship. Hop on board. I'd be happy to help," smiled Henry as he chewed on krill spilling from his mouth.

Penny untied the scarves from around her waist and returned them to Annika and Grace. She gave each of them a big hug as tears formed in her eyes. Penny was sad to see them go but she knew they belonged with their family as well, and she thanked them once more for all of their help. Annika and Grace carefully walked across Henry's back and settled down on his hump protruding from the icy water. The colony of penguins all waved good-bye as Henry slowly swam away from the ice floe being careful not to get the girls wet.

Henry safely navigated his way to the ship's dock and delivered the girls just in time for dinner. Annika kissed Henry on the cheek and said, "Thank you, Henry. Is there anything we can do for you?"

"No," said Henry, "this is your reward for being so kind to Penny when she was lost and all alone. You are truly good friends."

Annika and Grace waved good-bye to Henry and raced to their cabin giggling and holding hands. They were very hungry and tired from their adventure but too excited to sleep. The girls removed their winter clothing outside their cabin so Annika's parents wouldn't notice her missing mittens and Grace's missing hat. They left them in a heap in the hallway.

When they entered their cabin, it was still filled with sunshine, for the sun never sets here in the summer. The table was set for dinner and Annika's parents were waiting to hear all about their exploration. In the center of the table was a beautifully decorated birthday cake for Annika with a hand carved wooden penguin on top. Annika removed the penguin and licked its feet clean of frosting.

"I'll name her Penny," said Annika as her eyes met Grace's with a knowing grin.

She winked at Grace and put the wooden penguin safely in her pocket. Annika could not imagine a more perfect ending to her extraordinary birthday adventure.

Dedicated
to my granddaughter,

Annika Isabelle,

who inspires me every day
with her endless energy and
delightful sense of adventure.

CPSIA information can be obtained
at www.ICGtesting.com
Printed in the USA
LVHW071144181119
637665LV00007B/1589/P